Mao Zedong Selected Poems

Mao Zedong Selected Poems

Poems by Chairman Mao

Second Edition

Translated by Haiying Zhang

Translation copyright © Haiying Zhang 2006

ISBN: 978-0-9551672-2-5

www.haiying.org.uk

First published and printed in the United Kingdom in 2006

Reprinted in 2007

Little Bird Publishing

www.littlebirdpublishing.net

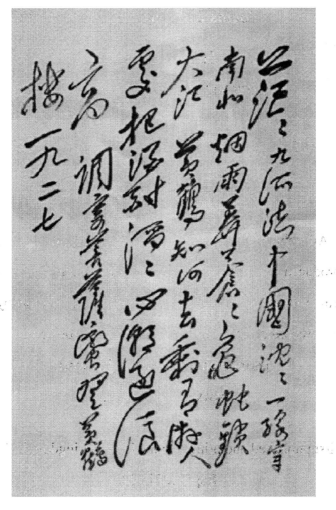

Chairman Mao's brush-writing

Poem 2: Yellow Crane Tower

目录 CONTENTS

Introduction

Mao Zedong (1893-1976) is not only a great political leader of China, he also wrote many poems in his life. His poems are all in the traditional Chinese verse style. Mao's poetry is bold and powerful, bringing history, reality and commitment together. He is a romantic poet deeply influenced by the Tang Dynasty poets Li Bai and Li He. This publication includes twenty of his poems both in Chinese and English with explanatory notes to each poem.

    1. Chang Sha (1925) This poem is usually considered to be one of Mao's best. Chang Sha is the capital city of Hunan province. Mao attended Hunan First Normal University in 1911 and left Chang Sha in1918. Orange Island (Line 3) is an island in the middle of the Xiang River, near Chang Sha.

    2. Yellow Crane Tower (1927) Yellow Crane Tower is a building on the bank of the Yangtze River in Wuhan (Hunan Province). It is famous in Chinese history and literary tradition. Its fame mainly comes from a poem written by Cui Hao in the early Tang Dynasty, "Yellow cranes have flown away with the ancestors, /Yellow Crane Tower alone still remains here".

3. Jing Gang Mountain (1928) Jing Gang Mountain is a mountain area at the border of Jiangxi province and Hunan province. Huang Yang Jie (Line 7) is the place where the Red Army defeated the KMT army after a fierce battle in the autumn of 1928.

4. Jiang Gui Conflict (1929) In 1929, Jiang Jieshi's KMT army began war with Feng Yuxiang and Yan Xishan's armies in north China. That is why Mao said, "Warlords in conflict again", and "a daytime dream" meaning that Jiang, Feng and Yan's ambitions were just dreams. Ting River is a river in Fujian. Both Longyan and Shanghang are cities in Fujian province in southeast China. In this poem, Mao expressed his hatred of the warlords' clash and praised the high spirits of the liberation peasants.

5. The Double Ninth Festival (1929.10) Double Ninth, also called Chongyang Festival, is a Chinese holiday. By tradition on 9th September (Lunar Calendar) each year, Chinese people would climb nearby mountains, look into the distance, and think about their family members who were travelling.

6. New Year's Day (1930.01) Ninghua, Qingliu, Guihua (Line 1) are all places in Fujian province. Wu Yi Mountain (Line 4) is in Fujian province.

7. On the Way to Guangchang (1930.02) Guangchang (Title) and Ji'an (Line 8) are cities in Jiangxi province. Gan River (Line 6) is a river flowing through Jiangxi province.

8. From Tingzhou to Changsha (1930.07) Tingzhou is a city in Fujian province. Changsha is the capital of Hunan province. At that time the Red Army tried to take Changsha, but failed. Huang Gonglue (1898-1931) was an important military leader of the Red Army who was killed in a battle in 1931.

9. Against the First Encirclement (1931) Zhang Huizan (Line 5), the KMT general who led the first Encirclement Campaign, was killed after being captured by the Red Army. Buzhou Mountain (Line 10) is a legendary mountain in Chinese tradition. It is said Buzhou Mountain was one of the four pillars supporting the sky. The God of Water, Gong Gong quarrelled with the God of Fire, Zhu Rong for some reason. Gong Gong was defeated and got so angry that he banged his head against the Buzhou Mountain. The Buzhou Mountain pillar supporting the sky collapsed, a huge hole appeared in the sky and heavy rain poured down from heaven, causing a huge flood on earth. Here Mao expressed his appreciation for Gong Gong's rebellious spirit.

10. Hui Chang (1934) Hui Chang is a place in Jiang Xi Province.

11. Lou Shan Pass (1935.02) This is a famous poem written during the Long March. Lou Shan Pass is a place in Guizhou Province, where a fierce battle took place.

12. Three Short Poems (1934-35) These three poems were written during the Long March period.

13. The Long March (1935.10) This poem was written toward the end of 1935 when the Long March was almost finished. Min Mountain is in the northwestern part of China. Here, Mao was glad to see all three Red Armies were together.

14. Liu Pan Mountain (1935.10) This was written in late 1935 after the Red Army almost finished the famous Long March. Liu Pan Mountain is in northwestern China. "Climb the Great Wall to be great (Line 3)" This famous quotation attracts millions of tourists visiting the Great Wall each year.

15. Snow (1936.02) This is a very famous poem by

Mao. In the first part, Mao praised the grandeur and beauty of northern China in winter. In the second half, Mao listed some of the greatest emperors in China, including Qin Huang (260 BC - 210 BC), the first emperor of China; Han Wu (156 BC-87 BC), the great Han emperor; Tang Zong (598-649), the second emperor of the Tang Dynasty; Song Zu (927-976), the emperor who started the Song Dynasty; and Genghis Khan (1162-1227), who united the Mongol tribes and founded the Mongol Empire.

16. The PLA Captures Nanjing (1949.04) In late April 1949, the PLA (People's Liberation Army) crossed the Yangtze River and captured the capital of KMT government Nanjing. Mao wrote this poem to celebrate this historical event. Xiang Yu (Line 6) is the hero who led the uprising that toppled the Qin Dynasty. After winning the war against the Qin Dynasty, Xiang Yu fought against Liu Bang for the control of China. Xiang Xu was defeated and killed himself in the Wu River.

17. Reply to Mr Liu Yazi (1950.10) Crimson Land (Line 1) is another way Chinese people call their own country. Yutian (Line 5) is a place in Xinjiang province in the far west of China, here means far away places.

18. Reply to Li Shuyi (1957.05) This is a poem written in 1957 by Mao Zedong to a female friend, Li Shuyi. In the translation, 'Poplar' actually means Mao's first wife Yang Kaihui, whose surname has the same sound as poplar; and 'Willow' actually means Li Shuyi's husband Liu Zhixun, whose surname has the same sound as willow. Yang (Poplar) and Liu (Willow) were both communist members. Yang was killed by the KMT in 1930, and Liu died in 1932 in a battle. In the poem Wu Gang is a man who according to Chinese legend, lives on the moon, and was forced by the gods to fell a laurel tree forever.

19. The Fairy Cave of Lu Mountain (1961.09) This poem was written as an inscription on a picture taken by Comrade Li Jin in 1961.

20. Ode to the Plum Blossom (1961.12) This poem encourages Chinese people to overcome difficulties during the hard times when the poem was written. It shows Mao's optimistic spirit.

Haiying Zhang
Westcliff-on-sea, 2006

1. 长沙

沁园春

独立寒秋，
湘江北去，
橘子洲头。
看万山红遍，
层林尽染；
漫江碧透，
百舸争流。
鹰击长空，
鱼翔浅底，
万类霜天竞自由。
怅寥廓，
问苍茫大地，
谁主沉浮？

携来百侣曾游。
忆往昔峥嵘岁月稠。
恰同学少年，
风华正茂；
书生意气，
挥斥方遒。
指点江山，
激扬文字，
粪土当年万户侯。
曾记否，
到中流击水，
浪遏飞舟？

(一九二五年)

CHANG SHA

To the tune of Qin Yuan Chun

In cold autumn, I stand.
Xiang River flows north.
At the tip of Orange Island,
I see all the mountains turned red,
Forests have been dyed;
The river is limpid,
Hundreds of boats are racing.
Eagles soaring,
Fishes flying,
For freedom they are seeking.
I doubt and ask the boundless earth,
Who is master?

With my friends, I travelled.
Times past and outstanding events, I recall.
We were young students,
With high spirits,
We were all learned
And impassioned,
Pointing to the mountains and lands,
We wrote emotional words.
All the past lords are nothing.
Do you still remember?
We hit the water in the middle of the river,
Flying boats slowed by waves?

(1925)

2. 黄鹤楼

菩萨蛮

茫茫九派流中国，
沉沉一线穿南北。
烟雨莽苍苍，
龟蛇锁大江。

黄鹤知何去？
剩有游人处。
把酒酹滔滔，
心潮逐浪高！

(一九二七年春)

YELLOW CRANE TOWER

To the tune of Pu Sa Man

Nine rivers run over China.
From north to south the skyline is heavy.
The rain is hazy,
Tortoise and Snake guard the river.

Where do the yellow cranes go?
Around the tower visitors.
I drink wine with huge waves,
They are lower than my heart tides.

(Spring 1927)

3. 井冈山

西江月

山下旌旗在望，
山头鼓角相闻。
敌军围困万千重，
我自岿然不动。

早已森严壁垒，
更加众志成城。
黄洋界上炮声隆，
报道敌军宵遁。

(一九二八年秋)

JING GANG MOUNTAIN

To the tune of Xi Jiang Yue

Down the mountain flags are waving,
Up the mountain drums are echoing.
We are surrounded by thousands of enemies,
But like the mountain we don't need to move.

Our defense has been so strong,
All our wills formed a wall.
Huang Yang Jie guns are roaring,
At night, enemies are fleeing.

(Autumn 1928)

4. 蒋桂战争

清平乐

风云突变，
军阀重开战。
洒向人间都是怨，
一枕黄粱再现。

红旗越过汀江，
直下龙岩上杭。
收拾金瓯一片，
分田分地真忙。

(一九二九年秋)

JIANG GUI CONFLICT

To the tune of Qing Ping Yue

Situation suddenly changed,
Warlords in conflict again.
Pouring hatred to all the world,
A daytime dream recurred.

Ting River, Red flag leapt,
Right to Longyan, Shanghang.
A golden piece of land tidied,
The loam is busily divided.

(Autumn 1929)

5. 重阳

采桑子

人生易老天难老，
岁岁重阳。
今又重阳，
战地黄花分外香。

一年一度秋风劲，
不似春光，
胜似春光，
寥廓江天万里霜。

(一九二九年十月)

THE DOUBLE NINTH FESTIVAL

To the tune of Cai Sang Zi

One grows old, Heaven never.
Each year Chong Yang,
Today Chong Yang.
Yellow blooms at Front are sweet.

Each autumn wind blows hard.
It's not yet spring,
Better than spring,
The vast sky and river are frosty.

(October 1929)

6. 元旦

如梦令

宁化，清流，归化，
路隘林深苔滑。
今日向何方，
直指武夷山下。
山下，山下，
风展红旗如画。

(一九三零年一月)

NEW YEAR'S DAY

To the tune of Ru Meng Ling

Ninghua, Qingliu, Guihua,
Narrow road, deep wood, sleek moss.
Where do we go today?
Right to the Wu Yi Mountain.
Down the mountain, down the mountain,
Flags blowing like a painting.

(January 1930)

7. 广昌路上

减字木兰花

漫天皆白，
雪里行军情更迫。
头上高山，
风卷红旗过大关。

此行何去？
赣江风雪迷漫处。
命令昨颁，
十万工农下吉安。

(一九三零年二月)

ON THE WAY TO GUANGCHANG

To the tune of Jian Zi Mu Lan Hua

The sky is all white,
Marching in snow, our will is stronger.
Mountain ahead,
We cross the great pass; red flags are rolling in the wind.

Where do we go?
The Gan River muffled by the snow.
We were told yesterday,
A hundred thousand peasants and workers go to Ji'an.

(February 1930)

8. 从汀州向长沙

蝶恋花

六月天兵征腐恶，
万丈长缨要把鲲鹏缚。
赣水那边红一角，
偏师借重黄公略。

百万工农齐踊跃，
席卷江西直捣湘和鄂。
国际悲歌歌一曲，
狂飙为我从天落。

(一九三零年七月)

FROM TINGZHOU TO CHANGSHA

To the tune of Die Lian Hua

In June, heavenly troops fight against foes,
Ten thousand metre-long ropes to tight foe masters.
Over the Gang River, a bit red,
Borrow troops from Huang Gonglue.

A million workers and farmers formed together,
Sweeping Jiang Xi, Hu Nan and Hu Bei.
The international song is stirring,
A whirlwind swoops from Heaven for me.

(July 1930)

9. 反第一次大 "围剿"

渔家傲

万木霜天红烂漫,
天兵怒气冲霄汉。
雾满龙冈千嶂暗,
齐声唤,
前头捉了张辉瓒。

二十万军重入赣,
风烟滚滚来半天。
唤起工农千百万,
同心干,
不周山下红旗乱。

(一九三一年春)

AGAINST THE FIRST ENCIRCLEMENT

To the tune of Yu Jia Ao

Trees in frost, red leaves are blooming.
Heavenly troops anger rising.
Mountains look dark, fog in Long Gang.
We are shouting,
At the front, we seized Zhang Huizan.

Enemies' huge troops came to Jiangxi again.
Half the sky wind and smoke coming.
Millions of workers and peasants are doing
The same thing.
Red flags down Buzhou Mountain chaotically flying.

(Spring 1931)

10. 会昌

清平乐

东方欲晓，
莫道君行早。
踏遍青山人未老，
风景这边独好。

会昌城外高峰，
颠连直接东溟。
战士指看南粤，
更加郁郁葱葱。

(一九三四年夏)

HUI CHANG

To the tune of Qing Ping Yue

Dawn is waking,
Don't say we are early.
Walking through all the mountains, we're young.
The landscape here is magnificent.

High mountains out of Hui Chang,
The peaks stretch east, Tung Ming.
Soldiers point out Guang Tung,
So green and alluring.

(Summer 1934)

11. 娄山关

忆秦娥

西风烈，
长空雁叫霜晨月。
霜晨月，
马蹄声碎，
喇叭声咽。

雄关漫道真如铁，
而今迈步从头越。
从头越，
苍山如海，
残阳如血。

(一九三五年二月)

LOU SHAN PASS

To the tune of Yi Qin E

West wind is strong,
Wide sky, wild geese cry, frosty morning moon.
Frosty morning moon,
Horse hoofs hurry,
Horns choke and sob.

The long great pass like iron,
Today we stride once again.
Stride once again,
The green mountain is like the sea,
Sunset blood.

(February 1935)

12. 十六字令三首

山，
快马加鞭未下鞍。
惊回首，
离天三尺三。

山，
倒海翻江卷巨澜。
奔腾急，
万马战犹酣。

山，
刺破青天锷未残。
天欲堕，
赖以拄其间。

(一九三四年到一九三五年)

THREE SHORT POEMS

To the tune of Shi Liu Zi Ling

Mountain,
Whipping my fast horse, not stopped by,
I look back, startled,
I am three feet three to the sky.

Mountain.
Seas upside down with huge waves,
Galloping,
Like millions of horses enjoying wars.

Mountain,
Remains sharp after piercing the sky.
The sky is nearly falling,
Supported by the mountain column high.

(1934-1935)

13. 长征

七律

红军不怕远征难，
万水千山只等闲。
五岭逶迤腾细浪，
乌蒙磅礴走泥丸。

金沙水拍云崖暖，
大渡桥横铁索寒。
更喜岷山千里雪，
三军过后尽开颜。

(一九三五年十月)

THE LONG MARCH

Qi Lv

The Red Army has no fear,
Mountains, rivers… we don't care.
Five mountains we fly over tiny waves.
We walk on Wu Meng clay balls.

Jinsha waves pat high cliff warm,
Dadu bridge its iron chains are cold.
Min Mountain snow smiles a thousand miles,
When the three Armies passing there.

(October 1935)

14. 六盘山

清平乐

天高云淡，
望断南飞雁。
不到长城非好汉，
屈指行程二万。

六盘山上高峰，
红旗漫卷西风。
今日长缨在手，
何时缚住苍龙？

(一九三五年十月)

LIU PAN MOUNTAIN

To the tune of Qing Ping Yue

Sky is high, clouds light,
Wild geese vanish to the South.
Climb the Great Wall to be great,
We have travelled twenty thousand miles.

Liu Pan Mountain is so high,
West wind plays with red flags.
Today we hold long cords in our hands,
When shall we bind fast the Gray Dragons?

(October 1935)

15. 雪

沁园春

北国风光，
千里冰封，
万里雪飘。
望长城内外，
惟余莽莽，
大河上下，
顿失滔滔。
山舞银蛇，
原驰蜡象，
欲与天公试比高，
须晴日。

看红装素裹，
分外妖娆。
江山如此多娇，
引无数英雄竞折腰。
惜秦皇汉武，
略输文采；
唐宗宋祖，
稍逊风骚。
一代天骄，
成吉思汗，
只识弯弓射大雕。
俱往矣，
数风流人物，
还看今朝。

(一九三六年二月)

SNOW

To the tune of Qin Yuan Chun

Scene in the north,
Ice for a thousand miles,
Snow flies ten times as far.
Look round the great wall,
Only whiteness;
The river all
Frozen at once.
White snake mountain dances
With wax elephants.
To measure with the sky,
When it is bright.

Look, a beauty in white,
She is so pleasing.
My country is charming,
She attracts countless heroes to bow.
It's a pity that Qin Huang, Han Wu
Couldn't write well;
Tang Zong, Song Zu,
They lacked good taste;
The son of Heaven, Genghis Khan,
Only knew hunting eagles.
All have gone,
Name those who are great,
Heroes are in our time.

(February 1936)

16. 人民解放军占领南京

七律

钟山风雨起苍黄，
百万雄师过大江。
虎距龙盘今胜昔，
天翻地覆慨而慷。

宜将剩勇追穷寇，
不可沽名学霸王。
天若有情天亦老，
人间正道是沧桑。

(一九四九年四月)

THE PLA CAPTURES NANJING

Qi lv

Yellow windstorm in Zhong Mountain,
Millions of troops cross the river.
Tigers and dragons are braver,
Everything is charged with great passion.

We must defeat our enemy with our courage,
Never seek fame like Xiang Yu.
Heaven grows old if it feels.
What the earth needs is justice.

(April 1949)

17. 和柳亚子先生

浣溪沙

长夜难明赤县天，
百年魔怪舞翩跹，
人民五亿不团圆。

一唱雄鸡天下白，
万方乐奏有于阗。
诗人兴会更无前。

(一九五零年十月)

REPLY TO MR LIU YAZI

To the tune of Huan Xi Sha

So slow Crimson Land's dawn comes,
Devils have danced a hundred years.
Kept apart five hundred million people.

Once the cock crows, the dawn comes,
Songs come from ten thousand corners
     including Yu Tian.
So excited are we the poets.

(October 1950)

18. 答李淑一

蝶恋花

我失骄杨君失柳，
杨柳轻扬直上重霄九。
问讯吴刚何所有，
吴刚捧出桂花酒。

寂寞嫦娥舒广袖，
万里长空且为忠魂舞。
忽报人间曾伏虎，
泪飞顿作倾盆雨。

（一九五七年五月十一日）

REPLY TO LI SHUYI

To the tune of Die Lian Hua

I lost proud Poplar you lost Willow,
Poplar and Willow soar up to Heaven,
Asking Wu Gang, what does he have?
Wu Gang takes out laurel wine.

Lonely Chang E spreads her vast sleeves,
Boundless sky, she dances only for good hearts.
Hearing a crouching tiger on earth,
Tears of joy fly like rain pouring down from bowls.

(May 11, 1957)

19.为李进同志题所
摄庐山仙人洞照

七绝

暮色苍茫看劲松，
乱云飞渡仍从容。
天生一个仙人洞，
无限风光在险峰。

(一九六一年九月九日)

THE FAIRY CAVE OF LU MOUTAIN

Inscription on a Picture Taken By Comrade Li Jin

Qi Jue

I see tough pines through twilight,
They are calm although messy clouds are in sight.
A fairy's cave was born by nature,
Boundless beauty is on perilous mountain peaks.

(September 9, 1961)

20. 咏梅

卜算子

风雨送春归，
飞雪迎春到。
已是悬崖百丈冰，
犹有花枝俏。

俏也不争春，
只把春来报。
待到山花烂漫时，
她在丛中笑。

(一九六一年十二月)

ODE TO THE PLUM BLOSSOM

To the tune of Po Suan Zi

Wind and rain see spring off,
Flying snow greets spring.
Cliff with a hundred metres of ice,
Branches in bloom are beautiful.

Never showing off,
Yet she heralds spring.
When the mountain is full of blooms,
She is there, smiling.

(December 1961)